ABOVE YOSEMITE

by ROBERT CAMERON

A new collection of aerial photographs
of Yosemite National Park, California

with text by Harold Gilliam

Cameron and Company, San Francisco, California

The floor of the valley in October.

(Opposite) Yosemite Falls.

(Opposite) Donohue Peak, looking toward Banner Peak and Mount Ritter.

Tuolumne Meadows.

TABLE OF CONTENTS

Such a book as this does not reach publication without more than the usual amount of
cooperation from many people. So, for their encouragement and expertise I thank the following:

Ansel Adams, Virginia Adams, Hatsuro Aizawa, Pat Akre, Ed Barwis, Robert Binnewies, Robert Derenzi, Robert Eckstrand, Nick Fiore, Ann Gilliam, John Goy,
John Graham, John H. Garzoli, Gladys Hansen, Alice Harth, King Huber, Suzanne Thomas Lawlor, Willi Maier, Dr. Mary Thomas Martinet, Set Momjian, Patricia O'Grady,
Kjell Qvale, Chris Redlich, Keith Schiller, Mary Vocelka, Clyde Wahrhaftig, Tom Wilhelm, and Robert Wormhoudt. And for his invaluable assistance throughout,
my special thanks to Armand B. "Herbie" Sansum of the National Park Service.

The pilots:

Andy Anderson, Ken Chase, Austin Dito, Andy Gemellaro, Keith Koch, Paul Moenning, Don Silva, Mel Taylor and Grant Wheatley.

Acknowledgment for Research Assistance is made to:

The Bancroft Library, National Air and Space Administration, San Francisco Public Library,
United States Geological Survey, Yosemite Natural History Association, Yosemite Research Library and Wilderness Press.

CAMERON and COMPANY
235 Montgomery Street   San Francisco, California 94104   415/981-1135

First Printing, 1983

©1983 by Robert W. Cameron and Company, Inc. All rights reserved.
Library of Congress Catalog Number: 83-90192
Above Yosemite ISBN 0-918684-20-X

Book design by
JANE OLAUG KRISTIANSEN

Typography by Reeder Type, Inc., Fremont, California   Color separation and printing by Dai Nippon Printing Co., Tokyo, Japan

YOSEMITE IN A NEW DIMENSION
by Harold Gilliam

What John Muir would have given to see Yosemite from above!

During his lifetime he saw it from every other perspective – hanging over the brink of Yosemite Falls, crawling behind the falls to see the moonlight through the water, exploring every square yard of the valley floor and rim, bounding up a talus slope while it was still shaking from the earthquake that created it, riding an avalanche, tracing the glacial pathways into the high country, scaling the peaks along the crest of the range.

He was driven by an insatiable desire to experience Yosemite and the Sierra Nevada from every conceivable vantage point, and to piece together the story of how this place came to be. Although in imagination he might have been able to picture the valley and the range as it would appear to an eagle high above, he was denied that ultimate view, the comprehensive perspective that has become available since humans have learned to travel in the sky.

More than a century after Muir first saw this valley, more than 60 years after Ansel Adams, following Muir's footsteps, first arrived here with his cameras and superlative artist's eye, Robert Cameron has focused his lenses on Yosemite from the air and has revealed this incredible region in a new dimension. Even if you have walked every foot of this terrain, you will see Yosemite here as you have never seen it before.

It is not hard to imagine what Muir's reaction would have been if he had been able to accompany Cameron in his plane or helicopter. When he first saw Yosemite Valley from the rim in July of 1869, he was overwhelmed by the sight. "I shouted and gesticulated in a wild burst of ecstasy," he wrote later. His alarmed dog stared at him and a startled black bear ran for cover. Later he made his way along the clifftop to the brink of Yosemite Falls:

> Never before had I seen so glorious a landscape, so boundless an affluence of sublime mountain beauty… The noble walls sculptured into endless variety of domes and gables, spires and battlements and plain mural precipices – all a-tremble with the thunder tones of the falling water.

Although he had come to the valley simply to see it and continue on his world travels, he decided to stay and learn more about this place of "sublime mountain beauty." He recorded his impressions in writings that convey an intensity of experience seldom paralleled in the literature of nature.

> As long as I live, I'll hear waterfalls and birds and winds sing. I'll interpret the rocks, learn the language of flood, storm, and the avalanche. I'll acquaint myself with the glaciers and wild gardens, and get as near the heart of the world as I can.

Cameron's views of Yosemite from the air provide a deeper understanding of Muir's greatest discovery: "Whenever we try to separate anything out by itself, we find it hitched to everything else in the universe."

Muir learned early in his Yosemite career that this valley could not be separated out by itself for study or enjoyment. In 1871 he wrote to a friend that he had been puzzling about the valley and its origin for three years:

> How did the Lord make it? What tools did He use? How did He apply them and when? I considered the sky above it and all of its opening cañons, and studied the forces that came in by every door that I saw standing open, but I could get no light. Then I said, You are attempting what is not possible for you to accomplish. Yosemite is the end of a grand chapter. If you would learn to read it go commence at the beginning. Then I went about to the alphabet valleys of the summits, comparing cañon with cañon, with all their varieties of rock structure and cleavage, and the comparative size and slope of the glaciers and waters which they contained. Also the grand congregations of rock creations were present to me, and I studied their forms and sculpture. I soon had a key to every Yosemite

> rock and perpendicular and sloping wall. The grandeur of these forces and their glorious results overpower me, and inhabit my whole being…

Seeing Yosemite from above, we are able not only to view its familiar rivers, meadows, waterfalls and granite monuments from totally new perspectives, we can "commence at the beginning" and see their origins in what he called the alphabet valleys of the summits, the grand congregations of rock creations. We can sense the processes of fire and ice whose sources are remote in time but whose visible signs are apparent in the far reaches of the Yosemite National Park and adjacent regions. And we experience these landscapes not as isolated features – as they are seen from the ground – but in their relations to each other, the beginnings of the whole "grand chapter" that culminated in the valley.

Although the chief authority on California geology in Muir's early years here, State Geologist Josiah Dwight Whitney, believed that Yosemite Valley was formed when the bottom of a shallow canyon dropped to great depths in some cataclysm, Muir knew better. He recognized the signs that Yosemite had been carved by moving ice, which had left its marks in striations in the granite walls where the Ice Age glaciers scraped by; in separate boulders or *erratics*, unrelated to the local bedrock, brought from afar by the moving ice; in burnished rock surfaces where the ice had polished the granite; and in moraines – ridges of rock debris left by glaciers.

Muir noted that there are many Yosemite-like valleys in the Sierra: "All Yosemites occur at the junction of two or more glacial canyons." The two principal glacial canyons that joined here are those of Tenaya Creek and the Merced River.

He also noted that ice was not the only force in shaping these landscapes. When the Pleistocene glaciers came down from the summits, they followed the canyons that had already been eroded by streams and rivers. And they sculptured the canyon walls in ways that were determined by the existing geologic structure of the rocks themselves. Yosemite's steep walls are the result not only of the work of water and ice but of joints in the granite that are oriented so as to produce a U-shaped valley rather than the usual V-shape.

Muir found that Yosemite's notable domes were results of the action of ice in uncovering the curving joints already present in the granite. Despite its great cutting power, he wrote, the ice only revealed the shapes immanent in the rock.

> In walking the sublime canyon streets of the Sierra, when we see an arch spanning the pine groves, we know that there is the section of a glacier-broken dome; where a gable presents itself, we recognize the split end of a ridge…If domes and cones appear, there we know the concentric structure predominates… Every carpenter knows that only a dull tool will follow the grain of wood. Such a tool is the glacier, gliding with tremendous pressure past splitting precipices and smooth swelling domes, flexible as the wind, yet hard-tempered as steel. Mighty as its effects appear to us, it has only developed the predestined forms of mountain beauty which were ready and willing to receive the baptism of light.

Some of the winter scenes you will see here may provide a foretaste of glaciers yet to come, future ice ages that will shape the landscape into entirely new yosemites – to be enjoyed, we may hope, by our distant descendants. The Yosemite we know may be not only the end of a grand chapter but the predecessor of more grand chapters yet to be written. The sweeping views of Sierra landscapes in these pictures you will see here provide insights into the vast sweeps of time as well.

> This grand show is eternal. It is always sunrise somewhere; the dew is never all dried at once; a shower is forever falling; vapor is ever rising. Eternal sunrise, eternal sunset, eternal dawn and gloaming, on sea and continents and islands, each in its turn, as the round earth rolls.

AERIAL ENTRY
TO THE VALLEY

There are three entrances to Yosemite Valley by road, all of them from the west. At left, Highway 120, the Big Oak Flat Road, comes over a ridge from the north and drops down to the level of the Merced River, providing tantalizing glimpses of the valley. Highway 140 from Merced comes up the river. Between the two roads as they converge is a flume carrying water from the small reservoir visible upstream. Near Bridalveil Fall, in the distance, was the lower limit of the last glaciation, which ended about 10,000 years ago. Earlier glaciations extended to El Portal, about nine miles downstream from here.

(Opposite) As the Big Oak Flat Road descends the slope toward the Merced River, it crosses Tamarack Creek and Cascade Creek just above their junction. The falls below are the Cascades, roaring here in the 1983 record spring runoff. On the highway just to the right of the bridges is a white patch of glacial till, a deposit of sand and gravel left by one of the older and larger glaciers that passed through here and ended at El Portal between 200,000 and 300,000 years ago.

(Opposite) *No temple made with hands can compare with Yosemite. Every rock in its walls seems to glow with life.**

The classic view of the temple opens up in front of you suddenly on the Wawona Road as you come out of the tunnel at Inspiration Point.

Here, looking east from 1000 feet above the point, you can see even more – including nearly every prominent feature of these ice-sculptured walls, as well as a glimpse of the high country beyond Half Dome.

*(All *italicized* passages in the picture captions are the words of John Muir.)

Looking downstream, you can see all three entrance roads: the Big Oak Flat Road dropping down the slope on the right, the Merced Road along the river, and the Wawona Road emerging from the tunnel to Inspiration Point on the left.

Coming out of the Wawona Tunnel at the right, visitors pause here, as do the sight-seers' "elephant trains," to gaze at the spectacular view of the valley visible from the car. What they see – and more – is visible on the next page.

CHIEF LANDMARKS (Opposite)

BV: Bridalveil Fall	ND: North Dome
C: Clouds Rest	RA: Royal Arches
CR: Cathedral Rocks	SD: Sentinel Dome
E: Echo Peaks	SR: Sentinel Rock
EC: El Capitan	TB: Three Brothers
HD: Half Dome	TC: Tenaya Canyon
MC: Matthes Crest	W: Washington
MR: Merced River	Column

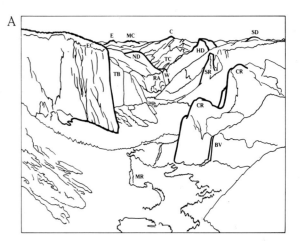

B

Nearly all of the upper basin of the Merced was displayed, with its sublime domes and cañons, dark upsweeping forests, and glorious array of white peaks deep in the sky, every feature glowing, radiating beauty that pours into our flesh and bones like heat rays from fire.

From 5000 feet above Inspiration Point, you can see not only the upper basin of the Merced (upper right, behind Half Dome), the source of one of the two great glaciers that entered at the head of the valley, but also the canyon of Tenaya Creek, pathway of the other glacier, entering the valley below Half Dome and Cloud's Rest.

B

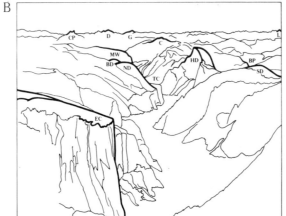

CHIEF LANDMARKS (Above and Opposite)

B: Banner Peak	KC: Koip Crest	R: Mount Ritter
BD: Basket Dome	L: Mount Lyell	RC: Rafferty Creek
BP: Bunnell Point	LC: Liberty Cap	SD: Sentinel Dome
C: Clouds Rest	LY: Little Yosemite	SK: Mount Starr King
CP: Cathedral Peak	M: Minarets	TB: Three Brothers
CR: Cathedral Rocks	MC: Mount Clark	TC: Tenaya Canyon
D: Mount Dana	ML: Merced Lake	TM: Tuolumne Meadows
EC: El Capitan	MW: Mount Watkins	WM: White Mountains
G: Mount Gibbs	ND: North Dome	
HD: Half Dome	NF: Nevada Fall	

C

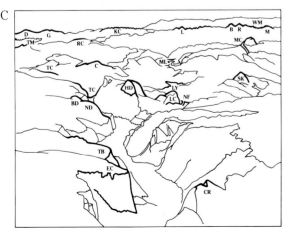

...When looking for the first time...the inexperienced observer is oppressed by the incomprehensible grandeur, variety and abundance of the mountains rising shoulder to shoulder beyond the reach of vision; and it is only after they have been studied one by one, long and lovingly, that their far-reaching harmonies become manifest. Then...the most complicated clusters of peaks stand revealed harmoniously correlated and fashioned like works of art – eloquent monuments of the ancient ice-rivers that brought them into relief from the general mass of the range.

Looking east from 16,000 feet above Inspiration Point on a winter day, you can see the courses of the ice-rivers that converged in Yosemite Valley and you can sense the atmosphere of the long glacial winter that produced the flowing ice. If this snow did not melt but continued to accumulate

year after year, century after century, it would turn to ice thousands of feet deep and carve out new landscapes as the old ice carved out these. That is precisely what may happen in the future, as it has happened many times in the past. (See the artists' version of Yosemite's geologic history on pages 126–128.)

In this view, the source of the Merced River, and of the ancient Merced glacier, is behind Mount Clark on the upper right, and you can trace the canyon leftward to frozen Merced Lake and down through Little Yosemite to Nevada Fall.

The great Tuolumne Glacier began on Mount Lyell, flowed north to Tuolumne Meadows and down the canyon of the Tuolumne River, out of the picture to the left. Part of the Tuolumne Glacier moved down through Tenaya Canyon to join the Merced Glacier below Half Dome and shape Yosemite Valley.

(Opposite) At midday in the fall, the shadow of Sentinel Rock moves across the meadows along the meandering Merced like the gnomon of a colossal sundial. Yosemite Lodge is in the trees at the lower left. The sand bars in the river indicate that the early snows on the rim have not melted sufficiently to raise the water level. The Old Village, razed in the 1950's owing to repeated flooding, was near the yellow maple at the shadow's edge, and the community center was moved to the present Yosemite Village near the foot of Indian Canyon, at left center. The Indian trail through the canyon has long since disappeared beneath repeated rock falls. The Ahwahnee Hotel is visible at the foot of the cliffs in the distance.

Yosemite Village is in the right center. Above it, nearly dry on this autumn day, is the gorge of lower Yosemite Falls, revealing a series of vertical "unloading joints." The joints are cracks where the granite has expanded as the pressure on it was released when erosion by water and ice removed gargantuan quantities of overlying rock.

The Merced River meanders here on top of lake sediments 2000 feet thick, the remains of lakes that covered the valley floor at various times after glaciers melted. The present floor of the valley stands at the level of the last lake. The lake was filled as the Merced and other inflowing streams deposited their loads of silt, sand, and gravel.

The Ahwahnee and its grounds in autumn gold, provided by meadow grasses and Kellogg oaks.

(Opposite) Although the Ahwahnee is one of America's great resort hotels, it was designed to be inconspicuous. Opened in 1927, it was built of native granite and wood and is screened from the surrounding valley floor by oaks, ponderosa pines, and incense cedars.

Rafting down the river on a summer afternoon, at the bend in the Merced near Ahwahnee Meadow, which appears at the upper left. The Merced here is flowing towards us, and like other rivers it creates beaches on the inside of big bends, where slower-flowing water and eddies deposit sand.

(Opposite) Royal Arches, above the Ahwahnee, illustrate the concentric jointing that produces both domes and arches under different circumstances. Water seeping into the joints freezes, expands and splits the rock. Similarly, spray from Yosemite Falls, entering joints in the granite, freezing, expanding and prying the rock loose, created the deep alcove in which the falls are located.

Nineteenth-century photographs show the area at the bottom of the picture inside the bend of the Merced River as open meadow with a few trees. (See page 22.) Now known as the El Capitan Picnic Area, it has been invaded by incense cedars, ponderosa pines, and black oaks until only a small portion of the original meadow remains.

(Opposite) The small pines growing in Sentinel Meadow, on the right, are part of a process that has greatly diminished the valley's meadows over the past century. The Ahwahneechees, a small tribe of the Miwok Indians who lived here before the "discovery" of the valley in the 1850s, burned and cleared underbrush and trees to keep the meadows open for hunting. Their successors used the meadows for grazing, and the partial elimination of the natural vegetation–sedges, grasses and broad-leaved plants–allowed some tree seeds to germinate.

When grazing was eliminated in the 1920s and the pasture fences were removed, tourists used the meadows for picnicking and car camping. Rangers dug ditches along the roads to keep the cars out, but the ditches began to drain the meadows and dry them out, permitting even more trees to move in. The National Park Service later followed varying policies of rooting the trees out or letting them spread to permit "natural" succession.

The net result of these practices was to diminish the original area of the valley's meadows by more than half. Recent park policy has been to conduct controlled burns at eight-year intervals, approximately the practice of the Ahwahneechees, who knew what they were doing.

Carleton E. Watkins, the pioneer photographer for whom Mount Watkins was named, may have taken this picture looking west down the valley from Union Point in the 1860s, about the time John Muir arrived. Cathedral Rocks dominate the upper center, and the brow of El Capitan appears at the upper right. Note the open quality of the forests, which have begun to overrun the meadows on the valley floor.

(Opposite) In a picture of approximately the same scene taken 120 years later, the forests have become far more dense, although Leidig Meadow (in the old picture just out of view at the lower right) has not yet been taken over by trees. Old rockfalls have become overgrown, and new ones have appeared.

COPYRIGHT, 1899, BY
H. G. PEABODY, BOSTON.

By 1899, the meadows of the upper valley had begun to sprout with the trees that today form tall groves. The Ahwahnee Hotel later was built below the arches on the left.

(Opposite) Part of the same scene in the 1980s. The partly overgrown talus slopes below the arches are composed of rock plucked from the wall over the ages by the processes of freezing and thawing and by earthquakes. Beyond the arches are other architectural shapes – buttresses, cornices, and Washington Column. Above them is North Dome and the white ridge of Clouds Rest. Behind Half Dome on the right in both pictures is Mount Clark.

24

A NASA U-2 view of the valley shot from an altitude of 12 miles by infrared photography, which shows greens as reds. At the upper left some bare granite reveals the course of Yosemite Falls, completely dry in this late summer view. Below on the valley floor are the rooftops of Yosemite Lodge. On the south, near, side of the valley, you can see the switchbacks of the Four-Mile Trail to Glacier Point, whose shadow is cast on the valley floor near Camp Curry (Curry Village). The Curry swimming pool is visible, as is the parking lot in Lamon's old apple orchard. The Ahwahnee Hotel is across the valley at the head of Ahwahnee Meadow, and to the left of the meadow among the trees is Yosemite Village. Slightly to the right of the Ahwahnee is the junction of Tenaya Creek and the Merced River. Vernal and Nevada falls are visible at the lower edge of the picture behind Half Dome, and above the falls the upper course of the Merced winds through Little Yosemite, headed by the cliffs of Bunnell Point. Below Half Dome in Tenaya Canyon the patch of white sand is the bed of Mirror Lake, nearly dry in late summer.

26

THE GRANITE MONUMENTS

The great Tissiak, or Half Dome, rising at the upper end of the valley to a height of nearly a mile, is nobly proportioned and life-like, the most impressive of all the rocks, holding the eye in devout admiration.

Like a hooded monk, Half Dome broods over the valley, and the sculptured textures of its base are revealed brilliantly in the morning light.

The stories told by those etchings in the granite are the stories of the ages – of magma welling up from the depths of the earth and crystallizing to granite below the surface; of millions of years of erosion of the overlying rocks, uncovering the granite. As the granite was slowly relieved of its titanic load, it expanded and cracked in unloading joints. It is these joints, vulnerable to attack by water and ice, that create the etchings and cause the granite to disintegrate, as layer after layer is peeled off like the skin of an onion.

(Opposite) *…A most noble rock, it seems full of thought, clothed with living light…steadfast in serene strength like a god.*

The sheer front of the dome was carved by the great Tenaya Glacier, which never quite reached the top. The darker areas and vertical streaks are the remains of mosses and lichens that grow where the water slides down the face from rain or snow melt.

On the horizon are the snow-covered cliffs of Buena Vista Crest on the left and Horse Ridge on the right. Glacial ice on the north sides of the ridges quarried away the slopes, leaving these escarpments.

(Opposite) Some of the most finely wrought glacial sculpturing in the park occurs here at the head of Little Yosemite Valley. On the right in the foreground are Cascade Cliffs. The cascade sliding directly down the cliff face is seldom seen at this volume attained in the spring of 1983.

Another cascade is on the Merced River where it skirts the foot of the cliffs. Immediately upstream on the same side of the river is Bunnell Point, with small seasonal cascade at the right. Bunnell Cascade, on the river below, is just out of sight. Far upstream you can see Merced Lake (which John Muir called Shadow Lake; it was the subject of one of his superb essays). On the crest of the range at the far right, just beyond snowy Mount Florence, is Mount Lyell, the highest point in the park.

The straight snowy line through forests at the upper left marks a grassy swale between two lateral moraines (ridges of boulders and gravel left along the sides of glaciers) that indicate the northern edges of glaciers that filled Little Yosemite Valley. The upper moraine was deposited about 100,000 years ago and the lower between 30,000 and 10,000 years ago.

The El Capitan Rock, regarded by many as the most sublime feature of the valley, is seen through the pine groves, standing forward beyond the general line of the wall in most imposing grandeur, a type of permanence. It is 3300 feet high, a plain, severely simple glacier-sculptured face of granite, the end of one of the most compact and enduring of mountain ridges, unrivaled in height and breadth and flawless strength.

Across the valley from here, next to the Bridal Veil, are the picturesque Cathedral Rocks, nearly 2700 feet high, making a noble display of the fine yet massive sculpture. They are closely related to El Capitan, having been eroded from the same mountain ridge…

Cathedral Rocks are on the south side of the valley in the foreground. To the right of El Capitan are the Three Brothers. The top of Yosemite Falls is visible over the Middle Brother and directly above, on the horizon, is monumental Mt. Hoffmann. To its right, at a greater distance, is Mount Conness.

The foot of El Capitan is buried in talus slopes hundreds of feet deep – rock that has been chipped off the cliffs above by ice forming in the crevices or by major earthquakes, which may have loosened enough rock to change the contours of the great monument in a very brief moment of seismic activity. The glaciers scraped the valley clean, but the talus has accumulated in the 10,000 years since the end of the last glaciation. Beyond El Capitan are the Three Brothers, topped by Eagle Peak, and across the valley is Sentinel Rock, with white Sentinel Dome above. Both Sentinel Dome and Half Dome were above the highest reach of the glaciers, but El Capitan was probably overswept by ice in an early glaciation.

(Opposite) Zooming in on El Capitan we pick out a team of ant-like rock climbers, who are ascending the wall over a period of several days. They are hauling up their packs on long ropes from the last ledge below. The leader is picking his way up the crevices, belayed by other members of the party, who secure the rope nearby to catch him if he should fall. The 3000-foot wall was first climbed in 1958, and many parties now ascend each summer.

The relatively horizontal white bands result from cracks in the older gray granite that were intruded by magma from the earth's hot innards when all this rock was still thousands of feet below the surface. The reddish-brown streaks are water stains and rust from iron oxides.

In the upper left is an overhang that is likely to be chipped loose and to fall within a few years – or a few millennia. Light-colored patches indicate recent chip-offs.

The persistence of life in a hostile environment is symbolized not only by the climbers but also by the pine growing in a crevice below them.

An early-day DC-3 passes the back of Half Dome. Park regulations now prohibit aircraft from flying low over the park (with some exceptions such as research and rescue craft).

(Opposite) In the foreground are the snow-capped twins, Mount Broderick (on the left) and Liberty Cap. On the horizon above Half Dome you see the battlements of the Mount Hoffmann ridge, which split the Tuolumne Glacier into two parts, one flowing beyond Hoffmann down the Grand Canyon of the Tuolumne to Hetch Hetchy, the other moving down Tenaya Canyon past Half Dome to Yosemite Valley.

(Opposite) Behind the southwest shoulder of Half Dome, the Merced River leaps free into the morning light at Nevada Fall. In line with the fall, two miles away, is the pyramidal granite monolith named for Thomas Starr King. Both Mount Starr King and Half Dome stood above the highest reach of the glaciers. Cascade Cliffs appear above Half Dome at the left.

On the skyline is the Clark Range, beginning on the left with the distinctive teapot-dome profile of Mount Clark. The peak was originally called the Obelisk owing to its narrow shape as seen from the north. The harrowing first ascent of Mount Clark in 1866 is described by Clarence King in his classic *Mountaineering in the Sierra Nevada.*

To the right of Mount Clark are Gray Peak, Red Peak, and Merced Peak, where John Muir in 1871 discovered his first living glacier. Also on the horizon, beyond Starr King, are Gale and Sing Peaks and Buena Vista Crest.

From high above Glacier Point, Half Dome appears to be not so much a dome as a tower, over-looking the pathways of the two glaciers that joined to shape Yosemite Valley – Tenaya Canyon to the left and the canyon of the Merced River to the right. Above Nevada Falls (Vernal is below, spotlighted here by a gap in a passing cloud), the Merced River meanders through the wooded valley of Little Yosemite.

To the left of Little Yosemite are the cliffs of Moraine Dome where concentric arcs of snow mark the successive moraines, or piles of rock, left behind as the last glacier melted back in several stages. The higher wooded area to the left of Moraine Dome is the basin of Sunrise Creek, bounded by Sunrise Mountain and Clouds Rest on the left.

On the far horizon are the peaks along the Sierra Crest: majestic Mount Conness on the far left, the spires of the Cathedral Range above Half Dome, pyramidal Mount Dana near the center.

The man in the lower right could take one step to oblivion. He is standing on the brink of the Half Dome overhang, looking straight down 4800 feet to Mirror Lake and across at the granite face of North Dome on the far side of Tenaya Canyon. The flaking of the top of the dome along the unloading joints is clearly visible.

Just right of the center of the picture is the course of Yosemite Falls, dry in October, and the shaded cliff beyond it. The buildings below it are Yosemite Village. Another sign of the season is the yellow maple on the valley floor. Beyond it, across the Merced River, the buildings of Yosemite Lodge are visible through the trees.

(Opposite) The glacial ice, overflowing from the Tuolumne Meadows region, went "swinging and swedging" down Tenaya Canyon, carving these walls into shapes determined by the joints already existing in the granite.

Across the canyon from Half Dome are its sister domes: Mount Watkins (nearest), Basket Dome, and North Dome (which was so-named when Half Dome was known as South Dome). The two granite knobs this side of Half Dome are the Quarter Domes. The sand bars of Mirror Lake are visible in the bottom, and on top of the far cliff, beyond Glacier Point, is the white summit of Sentinel Dome. To its right, down the valley, are Cathedral Rocks and, on the opposite side, the crest of El Capitan.

ABOVE THE FALLS

As it sways and swings in the wind, clad in gauzy, sun-sifted spray, half falling, half floating, it seems infinitely gentle and fine; but the hymns it sings tell the solemn fateful power hidden beneath its soft clothing.

The Bridal Veil shoots free from the upper edge of the cliff by the velocity the stream has acquired in descending a long slope above the head of the fall. Looking from the top of the rock-avalanche talus on the west side, about one hundred feet above the foot of the fall, the under surface of the water arch is seen to be finely grooved and striated, and the sky is seen through the arch between rock and water, making a novel and beautiful effect.

Under ordinary weather conditions the fall strikes on flat-topped slabs, forming a kind of ledge about two-thirds of the way down from the top, and as the fall sways back and forth with great variety of motions among these flat-topped pillars, kissing and splashing notes as well as thunder-like detonations are produced. The rainbows of the Veil, or rather the spray-and-foam-bows, are superb, because the waters are dashed among angular blocks of granite at the foot, producing abundance of spray of the best quality for iris effects…

(Opposite) In October Bridalveil plummets straight down from its notch, with little of the spring spray that gave it its name. On the left are Lower and Middle Cathedral Rocks, with the Gunsite between. On the right is the Leaning Tower, last and most difficult of the valley's principal monuments to be ascended by climbers, who first scaled its threatening overhang in 1961.

Water-loving big-leaf maples, kept damp by the spray from the falls, add autumn color to the slopes below.

Flying Fortresses buzz the valley over Bridalveil in World War II. The white streaks are rock avalanches that roared down the cliffs, perhaps precipitated by earthquakes at various times in the past. Note the trees invading Bridalveil Meadow (bottom center) and El Capitan Meadow (far left).

(Opposite) Here is Bridalveil 40 years later, emerging from its V-shaped hanging valley, with its full backdrop of cliffs and peaks. To the left and above the falls are Lower, Middle, and Upper Cathedral Rocks, and Taft Point on the valley rim. Above the forest belt is white Illilouette Ridge, and beyond it the pyramidal summit of Mount Starr King pointing toward Mount Clark, partly in shadow on the horizon.

(Opposite) On the left is Glacier Point, the only place on the valley rim accessible by road, where the scene is dominated by the dizzy drop to the valley floor 3000 feet below and by the spectacle of Yosemite Falls. Directly below Glacier Point are Camp Curry and Stoneman Meadow. The Merced River enters at the lower right, and just beyond the second bridge is the Ahwahnee Hotel. Beyond Ahwahnee Meadow is Yosemite Village. Portions of Yosemite Lodge are visible in the trees to the left of the bottom of the falls.

The white vertical streak to the left of the falls is where a slab of granite as long as a football field broke loose in the fall of 1980, killed three people and injured eight on the Yosemite Falls trail, which zigzags up the talus slopes. The path of crumbled white rock can be traced all the way to the bottom of the falls. Occasional rock falls are sobering reminders that geologic evolution continues and the processes of creation are never finished.

It has been argued that this is the world's highest waterfall, but the argument is pointless; it is the shape and form and motion of the water, in a dramatic setting, that give Yosemite Falls their distinction as a superlative. Even when the falls are totally dry in the autumn, the cliff face itself is one of the notable sights of the valley. To the right of the upper fall, near the center of the lighter-colored portion of the cliffs, is the Lost Arrow, a spire taller than the Washington Monument, standing free from the cliff in its upper portion, its summit just below the rim. The darker areas farther right are the Castle Cliffs, consisting of more abundantly jointed granite, with Indian Canyon beyond. The two shelves crossing the entire cliff indicate prominent horizontal jointing. The lower shelf to the right of the falls is John Muir's Sunnyside Bench, where he often camped while making his observations of the valley. To the lower right is part of Yosemite Village.

Yosemite Creek just before it plunges into the valley. A wooden footbridge is visible 100 yards above the head of the falls. Rocks peeling off the cliff to the left in slabs indicate unloading joints parallel to the surface. Yosemite Lodge is visible on the floor of the valley.

(Opposite) *A…nerve-trying view may be had from the rounded brow of the precipice close along-side the torrent as it leaps out into the air at the beginning of its descent. The view from here also extends from a point about 200 feet below the head, where the fall strikes a ledge and bounds out in characteristic comet-shaped masses all the way to the bottom…*

That ledge, which shoots upper Yosemite Fall as far as 100 feet out from the cliff, gives the water its free-falling character and its ability to descend in patterns constantly changed by the slightest breeze or spread across the cliff by gusts of wind.

Ribbon Fall, west of El Capitan, plummets 1612 feet—the highest sheer drop of any fall in the valley. However, it is normally nearly dry most of the year and even in the spring is difficult to see from the valley floor owing to its deep alcove, formed over the millennia as water from the spray penetrated fissures in the granite, froze, expanded, and chipped off flakes from the rock wall.

The picture on the right, taken through the slot in the alcove, shows Ribbon in a rare full flow as a result of extraordinary runoff during the spring of 1983. Ribbon was once called "Virgin's Tears," evidently in sentimental contrast to Bridalveil, across the valley.

(Opposite) *The Illilouette…in the exquisite fineness and richness of texture of its flowing folds…surpasses them all.*

Like Ribbon, Illilouette is best seen from the air owing to its relatively hidden location. Close views from below are available only to such intrepid mountaineers as Muir. It is visible from a distance at one or two points along the Vernal Fall Trail.

The trail visible here leads on the left to Nevada Falls; to the right over the bridge it ascends the ridge to Glacier Point.

A short distance above the head of Nevada Fall on the north side, the river gives off a small part of its waters, which forms a cascade in the narrow boulder-filled channel and finally meets the main stream again a few yards below the fall…The Commissioners came to regard these cascades as a waste of raw material, a damaging leak that ought to be stopped by a dam…That men such as the Commissioners should go into the business of improving Yosemite nature, trimming and taming the wild waterfalls properly to fit them for the summer tourist show, is truly marvelous American enterprise with a vengeance. Perhaps we may yet hear of an appropriation to whitewash the face of El Capitan or correct the curves of the Domes.

The rock dam Muir abominated is still there, blocking off the Liberty Gap Cascades, and is maintained by National Park Service officials, who fear that if it were not for the dam, the channel would be eroded until most of the river came through it, leaving Nevada Falls nearly dry. The streak on the cliff at the left indicates where a slab of granite has recently chipped off, revealing the white unweathered rock beneath; the shattered remains are on the talus slope below.

(Opposite) *The Nevada Fall is 600 feet high…Coming through the Little Yosemite in tranquil reaches, the river is first broken into rapids on a moraine boulder-bar that crosses the lower end of the valley. Already chafed and dashed to foam, overfolded and twisted, it plunges over the brink of the precipice as if glad to escape into open air. But before it reaches the bottom it is pulverized yet finer by impinging upon a sloping portion of the cliff about half-way down, thus making it the whitest of all the falls of the valley, and altogether one of the most wonderful in the world…*

SOUTH OF THE VALLEY

The South Fork of the Merced River comes down from snowy Gale and Sing Peaks to Wawona at the southern extremity of the park. The upper part of the green area is a meadow; the lower part is the park's only golf course. The high point at the right of the canyon is Raymond Mountain. Nearer on the same ridge is Wawona Point.

(Opposite) The historic Wawona Hotel was built on the site of an old cabin erected by Galen Clark, who settled here in 1855 and discovered the Mariposa Grove. Wawona was known as Clark's Station and for a time was the principal entrance to Yosemite.

Under the cloud at the far right in the picture opposite is the Mariposa Grove of big trees, the most visited of the Sierra's *Sequoia gigantea* groves. Although these trees are sometimes called *redwoods*, that name is more commonly given to the *Sequoia sempervirens* of the California coast. Pictured here is the Mariposa Grove's best known Sequoia, the Grizzly Giant, its dark foliage towering above neighboring firs.

(Opposite) High above Wawona looking toward the Sierra crest. The meadow at the center is the same one pictured on pages 52 and 53; to its left is the town of Wawona. Wawona Dome is the snowy eminence near the center of the picture and Wawona Point is on the right, across the valley of the South Fork of the Merced. On the horizon, the Clark Range is to the left, and the Mount Lyell group is above Wawona Dome, with Banner Peak and Mount Ritter slightly to the right.

On winter weekends at Badger Pass thousands of skiers ride the chair lifts to the top of the runs and slide down the white slopes at dazzling speed – or so they hope. Other visitors content themselves with a cup of hot buttered rum, gazing at the spectacle from the porch of the ski lodge.

(Opposite) After you become proficient on the bunny run, seen here on the far right, you are entitled to essay the steep drop immediately left or the long run down from the top of the ridge.

In the spring melting ice and snow form white patterns on the surface of Royal Arch Lake and on the intricate architecture of its granite walls. The lake is near the park's south boundary.

(Opposite) More venturesome skiers can leave the Badger Pass bowl entirely and explore pure realms of snow, sun and the incredible white beauty of the Sierra wilderness in winter.

Crescent Lake, near Wawona. The glacial bowl overflows into the South Fork of the Merced.

Red Peak and Merced Peak in the Clark Range. It was here that John Muir in October of 1871 (when there was much less snow than in this picture) discovered the first known existing glacier in the Sierra, confirming his unorthodox theory that the region had been sculptured by ice. Merced Peak was then known as Black Mountain.

I was… tracing the courses of the ancient glaciers that once poured from its ample fountains through the Illilouette Basin and the Yosemite Valley, not expecting to find any active glaciers so far south in the land of sunshine…The monuments of the tributary that poured its ice from between Red and Black Mountains I found to be the most interesting of them all; and when I saw its magnificent moraines extending in majestic curves from the spacious amphitheater between the mountains, I was exhilarated with the work that lay before me…The path of the vanished glacier was warm now, and shone in many places as if washed with silver…The sunbeams came streaming gloriously through the jagged openings of the col, glancing on the burnished pavements and lighting the silvery lakes, while every sun-touched rock burned white on its edges like melting iron in a furnace…Tracing the stream back to the last of its chain of lakelets, I noticed a deposit of fine gray mud on the bottom…It looked like the mud worn from a grindstone, and I at once suspected its glacial origin, for the stream that was carrying it came gurgling out of the base of a raw moraine that seemed in the process of formation… Cautiously picking my way, I attained the top of the moraine and was delighted to see a small but well-characterized glacier swooping down from the gloomy precipices of Black Mountain in a finely graduated curve to the moraine on which I stood.

After this discovery, I made excursions over all the High Sierra, pushing my explorations summer after summer, and discovered that what at first sight in the distance looked like extensive snowfields, were in great part glaciers, busily at work completing the sculpture of the summit peaks so grandly blocked out by their giant predecessors.

The National Park Service, reversing a long tradition of suppressing all fires in the park, now allows accidental blazes in remote areas, such as this one (opposite) on the South Fork of the Merced, to burn freely. Ecologists point out that historically, recurrent fires started by lightning or by Indians have played a vital role in the preservation of the forests. Without periodic burns, the brush and the leaf debris accumulate potential fuel to great depths and any accidental fires become so hot as to destroy the forest instead of merely clearing out the undergrowth.

The forest is also threatened when too much brush prevents the seeds of such trees as sequoias from reaching the ground and germinating. And the deer herds that once helped keep brush under control by grazing have been depleted as housing developments have invaded their winter range in the foothills, outside the park.

The view on this page shows a controlled burn deliberately started by park officials in the southern part of the park to burn off the undergrowth and restore a closer approximation to the natural regime.

TUOLUMNE COUNTRY

Dana Fork of the Tuolumne River, in the foreground, roughly parallels the Tioga Road, roaring down through cascades and waterfalls past the white tents of the Tuolumne High Sierra Camp and its parking lot. The road curves around Lembert Dome and crosses the river near the main Tuolumne campground in the trees on the left. It then skirts the south side of Tuolumne Meadows, passing by Fairview Dome on its way to Tenaya Lake. On the far horizon are Mount Hoffmann and Tuolumne Peak. As we have noted, part of the Tuolumne Glacier went to the left of this ridge and down Tenaya Canyon to Yosemite Valley. The greater part went to the right down the Tuolumne Canyon to Hetch Hetchy.

The dead trees in the foreground tell a story. Nearly all the trees in sight are lodgepole pines (named by Lewis and Clark in the Rockies when they observed the Indians using young trees for the poles of their buffalo-hide lodges). In cycles of decades, the lodgepoles are attacked by an insect, the lodgepole needleminer, which hollows out the needles. The trees appear to be dead, but young, healthy lodgepoles can survive three years of needleminer attacks, by which time the insect's natural enemies usually curtail its numbers and restore the balance, although old trees may not recover. During an infestation two decades ago, tons of malathion were sprayed aerially over this area to kill off the needleminer, setting off a great controversy, but more recent infestations have been left alone to let nature take its course.

(Opposite) *The big Tuolumne Meadows are flowery lawns, lying along the south fork of the Tuolumne River at the height of about 8500 to 9000 feet above the sea, partially separated by forests and bars of glacial granite. Here the mountains seem to have been cleared away or set back, so that wide-open views may be had in every direction…This is the most spacious and delightful high pleasure-ground I have yet seen. The air is keen and bracing, yet warm during the day; and though lying high in the sky, the surrounding mountains are so much higher, one feels protected as if in a grand hall.*

This, you might imagine, could be a low stage of the ancient Tuolumne Glacier moving past the foot of the Cathedral Range on its way to carve out the Grand Canyon of the Tuolumne. Actually, of course, it is simply the meadows buried under the deep white of a snowy winter. If the snow continued to accumulate, this would indeed be a resurrection of the old Tuolumne Glacier. Tracings on the snow in the right foreground are the meanderings of Delaney Creek as it emerges from the woods to the meadows and joins the Tuolumne, which is indicated by the larger curves. Visible peaks of the Cathedral range, left to right, are Unicorn, Coxcomb, Echo, Cathedral (with Tressider barely visible over its left shoulder), and Tenaya. The nearer of the domes at the right is Fairview.

(Opposite) The frozen meadows and the summit peaks, looking southeast. Lembert Dome is in the foreground, and the snowed-over bridge crossing the Tuolumne at the campground is visible at the far right. The canyon of Lyell Fork is at the upper left, leading toward rounded snowy Donohue Peak, and the sharp summits immediately to the right are Banner Peak and Mount Ritter, 15 miles away outside the park. The flat-topped peak in the nearer distance is Amelia Earhart, and the cluster of peaks immediately to the right includes Mount Lyell, at 13,114 feet the highest point in the park.

(Opposite) Below Tuolumne Meadows (which are near the far wooded area) is gemlike Tenaya Lake, seen here looking northeast. The lake is the source of Tenaya Creek, which flows into Yosemite Valley below Half Dome and joins the Merced River. In 1869 John Muir wrote in his journal:

August 8. Camp at the west end of Lake Tenaya. Arriving early, I took a walk on the glacier-polished pavements along the north shore, and climbed the magnificent mountain rock at the east end of the lake, now shining in the late afternoon light. Almost every yard of its surface shows the scoring and polishing action of a great glacier that enveloped it and swept heavily over its summit…This majestic, ancient ice-flood came from the eastward, as the scoring and crushing of the surface shows.

The new Tioga Road built in the 1950s is in the foreground; it continues along the left shore and the foot of Polly Dome, the "mountain rock" Muir climbed in 1869. The road continues eastward up the old glacial pathway, where the ice smoothed off the domes as it descended from Tuolumne Meadows. On the horizon to the left of center is Mount Conness.

Tenaya Lake, looking west. Polly Dome is on the right. Beyond the lake, on the far edge of the white area crossed by the road, is Olmsted Overlook. The principal path of the glacier was to the left of that area down Tenaya Canyon, beneath Clouds Rest (the pointed ridge to the left), and below Half Dome (center) where it converged with the Merced Glacier. On the near ridge to the left is pointed Tenaya Peak and beyond it, on the horizon, Buena Vista Crest and Horse Ridge.

The lake was named for the chief of the Indians who were driven from the valley by American soldiers in 1851 and fled to this lake, where they surrendered. The chief was taken prisoner and tied to a tree to prevent his escape.

A fine monument the old man has in this bright lake and likely to last a long time, though lakes die as well as Indians, being gradually filled with detritus carried in by the feeding streams, and to some extent also by snow avalanches and rain and wind. A considerable portion of the Tenaya basin is already changed into a forested flat and meadow at the upper end, where the main tributary enters from Cathedral Peak.

Frozen Tenaya Lake in winter, looking south toward the valley. Quarter Domes are downslope from Clouds Rest; Half Dome is in the center; and white Sentinel Dome, is beyond the valley on the right.

Over the Cathedral Range looking north to Tuolumne Meadows and the Sierra crest beyond, dominated by Mount Conness on the left and Mount Dana on the right. In the left foreground is Tressider Peak, whose sharp outcrops of granite and soft soil, like those of other nearby peaks, indicate that it was not overridden by the glaciers. Beyond Tressider is Upper Cathedral Lake, and above the lake is Cathedral Peak. Echo and Coxcomb peaks are in the right foreground. Lembert Dome, just above the center of the picture, has obviously been overridden by ice, as have all the rounded lower domes. The long parallel lines across the foreground granite are joints in the rock, not ice-cut grooves.

Lyell Fork in winter, recalling the glaciations that swept the range during the Ice Age. The 50-mile Tuolumne Glacier, which originated here, was the longest in the Sierra. Banner Peak and Mount Ritter are at the far left, and Mount Lyell is the snowiest peak in the middle of the picture.

(Opposite) The two main watersheds in the national park are the Merced in the south and the Tuolumne in the north. The real head of the Tuolumne is Lyell Fork, route of the John Muir Trail, which is visible near the center of the picture and extends south for 200 miles to Mount Whitney, through wilderness nearly all the way. The trail leaves the park at Donohue Pass, just beyond the rounded snowy summit of Donohue Peak, and continues through the country dominated by Banner Peak and Mount Ritter, whose summits are visible beyond the pass. Mount Lyell is just out of the picture to the right.

One of the best general views…is from the top of Fairview Dome [center]…the summit is burnished and scored like the sides and base, the scratches and striae indicating that the mighty Tuolumne Glacier swept over it as if it were only a mere boulder in the bottom of its channel…A few erratic boulders, nicely poised on its crown, tell an interesting story. They came from the summit peaks 12 miles away, drifting like chips on the frozen sea, and were stranded here when the top of the monument emerged from the ice…

(Opposite)…We find immense slate mountains, like Dana and Gibbs, resting upon a plain granite pavement, as if they had been formed elsewhere, transported and set down in their present positions, like huge erratic boulders. It appears, therefore, that the loftiest mountains as well as peaklets and pinnacles of the summit region are residual masses of the once solid wave of the whole range.

The dark reddish-brown of Mounts Dana and Gibbs, on the Sierra crest east of Tuolumne Meadows, contrasts strikingly with the dominant white granite of the Sierra, exemplified here by low Lembert Dome. Like other dark summits, these two peaks are remnants of the old metamorphic rock into which the granite magmas were intruded from below. Ultimately the granites were exposed by erosion of ice and water, revealing today's "Range of Light."

Hikers on Lembert Dome pass erratic boulders dropped here by the last glacier. The granite is splitting and chipping along the planes of the unloading joints.

(Opposite) Lembert Dome is a *roche moutonée* or *sheep rock*. Glacial ice overode it from the right, plucking off the downstream side to form sharp cliffs.

The white roof of the stables is visible at the left, and the Tuolumne Meadows campground is in the trees at the bottom. Dog Lake appears over the right top of Lembert Dome, and the lodgepole-pine forest beyond is growing on a massive ground moraine left by the glacier. Mount Conness is in the center, and White Mountain is the rounded summit to the right.

The lower end of Tuolumne Meadows, looking west, just before the river drops down into the Grand Canyon of the Tuolumne. Meandering Delaney Creek joins the river from the right. Compare with winter scene on page 66. At the upper left is Tuolumne Peak, the northerly end of the Hoffmann ridge.

(Opposite) Separating the national park's two main watersheds, the Tuolumne and the Merced, is the Mount Hoffmann ridge, seen here looking northeast over the Tuolumne to Mount Conness. The sharp outcrops on the summit of Hoffmann indicate that the glacial ice never reached this height. On July 26, 1869, John Muir wrote in his journal:

Ramble to the summit of Mount Hoffmann, eleven thousand feet high, the highest point in life's journey my feet have yet touched. And what glorious landscapes are about me, new plants, new animals, new crystals, and multitudes of new mountains far higher than Hoffmann towering in glorious array along the axis of the range...The rock [of the peak] is mostly granite, with some small piles and crests rising here and there in picturesque pillared and castellated remnants of red metamorphic slates...Great banks of snow and ice are piled in hollows on the precipitous north side forming the highest perennial sources of Yosemite Creek.

The broad gray summit is barren and desolate-looking in general views, wasted by ages of gnawing storms; but looking at the surface in detail, one finds it covered by thousands and millions of charming plants. How boundless the day seems as we revel in these storm-beaten sky gardens amid so vast a congregation of onlooking mountains.

The Grand Canyon of the Tuolumne in winter. From Tuolumne Meadows, below Dana and Gibbs at the upper right, the Tuolumne Glacier cut through granite, with joints that were oriented in such a way that produced a V-shaped canyon rather than the U-shaped valley created in Yosemite. Not until it reached Hetch Hetchy below did the glacier slice into granite that produced Yosemite-like walls.

(Opposite) Below Tuolumne Meadows, which appear at the upper right, the Tuolumne River cuts deeply into the Grand Canyon of the Tuolumne and the narrows of Muir Gorge at the bottom. Register Creek enters the gorge on the left, and the deep tributary farther upstream on the left is the canyon of Return Creek.

The highest peaks on the horizon are Mount Conness to the left and Dana and Gibbs on the right.

A NASA infrared view of Hetch Hetchy Reservoir from 12 miles up. The Tuolumne River is impounded by San Francisco's O'Shaughnessy Dam, which is visible at the far right, along with part of the lower course of the river.

This 1900 photograph of Hetch Hetchy Valley can convey little of the lushness and color of what Muir called the "Tuolumne Yosemite...a wonderfully exact counterpart of the Merced Yosemite, not only in its sublime rocks and waterfalls but in the gardens, groves and meadows of its flowery park-like floor."

Despite the protests of Muir and his Sierra Club, the valley was dammed to supply water and power for San Francisco, even though it lay entirely within the national park.

(Opposite) Looking north across Hetch Hetchy just above O'Shaughnessy Dam. Tueeulala Falls on the left, Wapama Falls on the right.

Before Hetch Hetchy Valley was dammed in the 1920s, proponents of the dam argued that visitors would flock to enjoy the beautiful lake. But the reservoir must be drawn down most of the time to supply water and flood-control capacity, and the banks are hardly inviting. Hetch Hetchy has few visitors.

(Opposite) Looking east up Hetch Hetchy Reservoir; white Mount Conness on the center skyline. The wooded peak nearer left is Rancheria Mountain.

YOSEMITE GEOLOGY: AN AERIAL ASPECT

There are few more spectacular drives on the continent than the Tioga Road down the steep eastern slope of the Sierra and few that offer more penetrating insights into the geologic processes that shape a region. Eastward from Tuolumne Meadows, the road crosses the park boundary at Tioga Pass, at 10,000 feet the highest automobile pass across the range. Then it skirts Tioga Lake, and curves to the right around the base of Tioga Peak.

In the years since Muir did his pioneer work in Sierra geology, the accumulation of geologic data has verified most of his major points and added some corrections and refinements. In the 1920s François Matthes of the U.S. Geological Survey, following up on Muir's work, determined that there had been not one glacial age in the Sierra, as Muir had assumed, but three. Only the last of the three, however, had left readily visible evidence. Some points on the Yosemite rim had never been entirely overridden by ice. Matthes also described the uplifts of the range and the extent of successive glaciations, with results pictured in the paintings reproduced on pages 126-128.

In the early 1980s Clyde Wahrhaftig of the University of California and the U.S. Geological Survey, making a geologic map of the Yosemite region, summed up the more recently developed knowledge of the Sierra. The plate-tectonic theory, which has revolutionized the science of geology, explains that the crust of the earth is composed of separate plates that move, over periods of millions of years, in response to pressures from below. The East Pacific plate and the North American plate have moved toward each other in a continuing collision along the west coast of the continent. The edge of the Pacific plate was submerged or "subducted" under the North American plate. As the leading edge of the eastward-moving oceanic plate was driven deeper beneath the continental plate, it became hot enough to create molten magma. Part of the magma erupted as volcanoes. The rest crystallized below the surface into various types of granite, as happened beneath the ancestral Sierra Nevada, a low range composed mostly of the dark metamorphosed layers of ancient sea beds.

Subsequent erosion removed the volcanoes and most of the metamorphic rocks and exposed the light-colored granite that caused Muir to call the Sierra the Range of Light. But here and there, peaks of the dark slates and other metamorphic rocks of the ancestral Sierra remain as "roof pendants," particularly in Yosemite around the head of the Tuolumne Meadows.

In the last twenty million years the Sierra slowly rose, tilting westward, and the area immediately east of it dropped, creating the steep eastern slope, or fault scarp. The increasing height of the range caused the rivers and streams to flow more swiftly and intensified their cutting power, creating the deep canyons in the western slope.

Beginning two or three million years ago, the earth grew cold. Along the Sierra crest, high snowfields deepened and compacted into ice—great glaciers that moved ponderously down the valleys, shaping the terrain as they did so.

Elaborating on Muir's point that the ice revealed the shapes already present in the basic structure of the granite, Wahrhaftig pointed out that the structure itself was largely determined by expansion of the granite as the immense load of overlying rock thousands of feet deep was removed by erosion. As we have noted, the cracks created as the granite expanded are unloading joints, more vulnerable to erosion than the solid rock between them. It is these joints that determined the shapes that emerged from the ice. From time to time the glaciers would melt, leaving most of the range free of ice, and return again when the climate grew colder. Wahrhaftig believes that there have been many more glaciations than either Muir or Matthes suspected – at least five and probably as many as ten or eleven, with the last one ending only 10,000 years ago, and others, perhaps, in store for the millennial future.

Beyond Tioga Lake the road descends quickly to Ellery Lake at the foot of Dana Plateau. At the upper right of this view is the characteristic dark pyramid of Mount Dana. The gray spot in the snow just below the peak is part of the ice of the Dana Glacier, a diminutive counterpart of the Ice Age glacier that carved out the cirque above, here nearly filled with snow. The U-shaped rock mass protruding through the snow just below the visible ice is the moraine – loose rock quarried by the ice from the cliffs and deposited at the glacier's terminus.

Muir and other early geologists believed that the Sierra's present glaciers were remnants of the Ice Age glaciers that shaped the range, but more recent evidence seems to indicate that those ancient glaciers had completely melted by about 10,000 years ago and that the existing glaciers were formed during the Little Ice Age – a period of abnormally cold climate that lasted for several centuries and ended only in the mid-1800s. During the warm climate of the past century the existing Sierra glaciers have receded.

Long before the Ice Age, and long before the Sierra was elevated to its present height, the range, as we have noted, consisted of rolling hills a few thousand feet in elevation. Most of the old rolling contours have been eroded away, but a few examples remain. Hikers who scramble up steep slopes are often surprised to emerge at the top on these ancient tablelands such as the Dana Plateau.

In the millennial spans of geologic time, the edges of the plateau are being worn away on all sides by water and ice. Similar plateaus appear near the crests of many peaks along the spine of the range, including Mount Whitney, 120 miles to the south.

Another story revealed in this picture predates both the glaciers and the plateau topography. The reddish rock is a roof pendant, a remnant of the ancestral Sierra, "cooked" or metamorphosed by the hot magma intrusions. The magma cooled and crystallized into granite. Here we see a line of contact between the gray granite and the reddish metamorphics, beginning at the lower left and continuing diagonally up across the ice-carved cliffs and the plateau itself.

Below Ellery Lake the Tioga Road edges along some dizzying glacial cliffs and emerges here to cut across the long talus slopes on the north side of Lee Vining Canyon. The canyon itself was carved into this typical U-shaped glacial valley by masses of moving ice, including the glacier that originated, as we have seen, in the cirques above on Mount Dana. Most of the rock visible here is granite, with some of the reddish metamorphics in the foreground.

In the distance to the east are Mono Lake and the long line of the Mono Craters, some of which erupted only a few hundred years ago and could spout off again in the not-too-distant future. On the far horizon are the White Mountains, including Boundary Peak, at 13,143 feet the highest point in Nevada and about 100 feet higher than Mount Dana.

Looking back up Lee Vining Canyon, with Dana Plateau at the top left and Tioga Peak just right of center. The upper part of the Tioga Road cuts across the base of Tioga Peak at approximately the top level of the main glacier. At the bottom it parallels an access road leading to campgrounds in the canyon bottom. The cirque in the near side of Dana Plateau was cut by a side glacier that pushed some morainal rocks and boulders over the edge of the canyon in the slide visible here, but it did not extend far enough to join the main glacier, which about half filled Lee Vining Canyon at this point.

At the bottom of Lee Vining Canyon the glacier left two very clearly visible lateral moraines, nearly as level as the sides of a plowed furrow. The road runs along the bottom of the moraine on the left, which almost appears to be a man-made embankment. The right moraine is overgrown because it is on the shady south side of the canyon, where more water is available. The series of mounds extending into the canyon, beginning with the one at the lower left, are recessional moraines left by the glacier at points where it paused temporarily when it was receding at the end of the last Ice Age. The moraines acted as dams, creating a series of small lakes which have since been filled by sediments brought down by Lee Vining Creek and converted to meadows. The meadows in turn are being converted to forests by the invasion of trees in areas where the meadows are drying out.

Note the dust storm on the far side of Mono Lake, where the wind whips across alkali flats exposed by the drawdown of the lake as its tributaries, including Lee Vining Creek, are channeled into the Los Angeles water system.

Reddish Mount Lewis, like Dana and Gibbs a few miles north, is one of the ancient roof pendants. It is composed principally of old sea-bed sediments metamorphosed by the intrusion of the magma, which crystallized into these light gray granite rocks in direct contact with the metasedimentary reds. The small body of water at the base of Mount Lewis is Parker Lake, impounded behind the large terminal moraine of the glacier that descended to the right of Lewis. Grant Lake, beyond, is in a hollow left by the parallel lateral moraines plowed up by the glacier that came down the canyon of Rush Creek to the south. Visible in the distance, just above the summit of Mount Lewis, are the lateral moraines of Lee Vining Creek shown in the preceding picture.

A dying lake in Northern Yosemite. The creek, pale with sand and silt derived from some ample upstream source, deposits its load as it enters the lake from the left, building natural levees on both sides. The levees lengthen until they carry the stream in its own channel entirely through the lake. The reddish-purple colors are organic material, such as algae and mosses, growing in the shallow water alongside the expanding levees. In time the lake will become entirely filled with the sediment and turn to meadow.

(Opposite) Here we move from the dry east side of the range to the cool alpine country in the park north of Hetch Hetchy. Ardeth Lake is a typical glacier lake in a high basin scooped out by the moving ice that passed along the flanks of Mahan Peak at the left but did not overtop the summit. The small lakes to the right are nearly 1000 feet lower in Jack Main Canyon.

The same process visible in the preceding picture is much further advanced here in Northern Yosemite's Thompson Canyon, looking southwest. The creek has developed several meandering channels where it deposits the sediment that will eventually convert it into a dry meadow. Over the millennia, all of the Sierra's glacial lakes tend to become meadows in similar fashion, the shallow ones by this process of levee building, the deeper ones by the growth of a delta where the stream enters and deposits its sediment directly, filling the lake from the head down. In effect the lakes are footprints of the late glaciers, and they shrink as the time since the last glaciation lengthens. Although it may be discouraging to think that these gems of the mountain landscape are vanishing, it may be possible to take consolation in the possibility that a future ice age will scoop out beds for new lakes, and the entire process will be repeated: birth, death, and new life.

So far we have talked about the Sierra granite as if it were the result of a single intrusion of magma bubbling up from the hot contact between the Pacific and continental plates of the earth's crust and crystallizing below the surface. What actually happened was far more complex. The intrusions came at various times and intruded one another in complicated ways, as this view in Northern Yosemite indicates.

That's Mahan Lake in the foreground, with the green meadows of Jack Main Canyon immediately to the southwest. Andrews Peak is in the center looking down on the meadows, and to the left of the peak are Middle and Upper Branigan Lakes. The wooded peak beyond is Mount Gibson and on its far side is the Grand Canyon of the Tuolumne. The oldest rock visible here is the light granite in the foreground. Long after the magma crystallized into granite, its parallel joints were invaded by another intrusion of magma that became diorite, resulting in these visible dikes of dark diorite that provide the prominent zebra-stripe pattern. Much later there were more intrusions of magma resulting in even darker diorite visible around Andrews Peak, Mount Gibson, and the Branigan Lakes. The fourth intrusion resulted in the lighter granodiorite visible to the right of Mount Andrews and around Lake Vernon, just beyond.

All this was taking place long before the ice came and (along with water) eroded away the overlying rock to expose the granite. The youngest feature of this landscape, which geologically speaking developed only yesterday, is Mahan Lake, impounded by a post-glacial landslide visible at the far end. To grasp the events represented by these rocks of different origins is to see the Sierra in a vastly expanded dimension of time.

Long after the magmas crystallized below the surface to form the granites and other igneous rocks visible in the previous picture, to the north of Yosemite – both in the Sierra and in the Cascades – other magmas originating in the collision of tectonic plates reached the surface and were erupting as volcanoes. This view, slightly north of the park, shows vividly the boundary between the Yosemite-type granites in the foreground and the bedded volcanic rocks. Beyond Relief Reservoir in the center of the picture the volcanics predominate, and a close look at the unvegetated mountainsides shows the layer-cake effect of the bedded lava and tuff (solidified volcanic ash). The Sonora Pass road is visible above and to the left of the reservoir. Although the volcanoes are not currently erupting in the Sierra, the magmas are still reaching the surface in the Cascade Range to the north, most recently at Mount St. Helens.

(Opposite) Part of the east face of Slide Mountain in northern Yosemite came roaring down into Slide Canyon with such force that it crossed the canyon and went part way up the far side. The slide, which is a quarter-mile wide, was probably triggered by a great earthquake, and the lack of vegetation on it indicates a geologically recent origin. Some geologists have argued that it came down in the great quake of 1872 (which John Muir observed in Yosemite Valley with mixed fear and delight). More recent evidence suggests that it may be several hundred years old.

This view of Black Bear Lake (below) and Bigelow Lake, just north of the park boundary, tells a story that begins 200 million years ago when this area was the floor of the Pacific. The layers of sand and clay on the sea bottom, under intense pressure from the weight of layers laid down above them, consolidated and became sedimentary rocks. Under further pressure these layers were bent and folded. Intense heat from below "cooked" them into three types of metamorphic rock: quartzite, schist, and marble. The quartzite is visible here as the grayish rock on the near side of Bigelow Lake. The schist is the brown rock on the cliff beyond Bigelow, and the marble is visible in lighter gray patches at the upper right and upper left.

Next, magma from tectonic pressures below was squeezed up into the cracks in these rocks and was crystallized as gabbro, the dark-brown rock on the upper right and in the cliff immediately above Black Bear Lake. Then the entire complex of rocks was invaded by another mass of magma, which crystallized as granite to form the light-gray surface appearing through the snow at the lower right. All of the rocks were far under ground when these events occurred, and in the latest chapter of the story they appeared on the surface after the overlying strata were eroded away by flowing water and moving ice, which at the end of the chapter scooped out the two lakes.

We can anticipate that the next 200 million years will be equally eventful.

This surprising view of Mount Starr King from the northeast reveals it not as a single cone, as it appears from other directions (see page 36) but a series of granite domes that were never overridden by the glacial ice. The summit is the farthest right of the three adjacent barren domes in the center. The lines etched on the domes are the unloading joints resulting from the expansion of the granite as the overlying burden of rock was eroded away. As the dome-shaped layers peel away with erosion, they crumble and form the talus slopes below. Other domes in this view were similarly formed, not by glacial erosion but by the unloading process as the overburden was removed. Across the middle of the picture is the valley of Illilouette Creek, which flows to the north, or right, toward Illilouette Falls and Yosemite Valley. Beyond Illilouette Ridge in the distance is the smoke of a management-controlled fire. (See page 63.)

Existing glaciers are found near the crest of the range on the shady north slopes, where there is less heat from the sun and where the snow collects over the centuries until it is solidified into ice. In this view of the north sides of Mount Lyell and Mount Maclure, there are three glaciers beneath the snow: two on Lyell, separated by the diagonal ridge, and one immediately to the right of the summit of Maclure. At the foot of the latter glacier in August of 1872, when there was less snow than appears here and the ice was readily visible, John Muir, assisted by Galen Clark, placed a series of stakes to determine whether the ice was moving. He returned in October and found, contrary to the prevailing dogma of Josiah Whitney of the State Geological Survey, who insisted there were no existing glaciers in the Sierra, that it was indeed a "living glacier" and its center was moving downstream about an inch a day.

(Opposite) Sawtooth Ridge, along the park's northern boundary, is an arête (a knife-edge crest), composed of Cathedral Peak granite, which characteristically erodes into such pinnacles as these when the sides of the ridge are glaciated. The type of granite takes its name from the Cathedral Range south of Tuolumne Meadows (see page 71), where similar pinnacles are visible on Cathedral Peak itself, Unicorn Peak, Cockscomb, and Echo Peaks.

(Opposite) Glacier-created waves on the landscape are visible in this view of Harden Lake, on a shelf above the Grand Canyon of the Tuolumne (which is just out of the picture at the bottom). The top of the 3600-foot-deep Tuolumne Glacier spilled over the edge of the canyon onto this shelf and left the moraine that impounded the lake and constitutes its far shore. The meadow to the right is a filled-in lake left from an earlier glaciation, which piled up the moraine that parallels the Harden moraine and extends into the meadow.

In the shallow canyon beyond is the Middle Fork of the Tuolumne River, and in the woods on the far side is White Wolf Lodge, both hidden by the trees. The Tioga road skirts the base of the barren cliffs in the distance. The cliffs are the walls of cirques carved out by small glaciers. Because of their relatively low elevation of about 8,000 feet, the glaciers did not contain enough ice to gouge out deep cirques and were able only to scrape off a small quantity of rock. Their moraines at the foot of the cliffs impounded small Siesta Lake, which is alongside the Tioga Road, also both hidden in the forest. On the far horizon, beyond Yosemite Valley, is Buena Vista Crest, near the park's southern boundary.

The peaks east of the Sierra crest, in the land of little rain, offer striking displays of the colors of the basic rock, whose hues are less visible on the forested west side. Dunderberg Peak, overlooking the Mono Basin beyond, is part of the same belt of reddish metamorphic rock we have seen on Dana and Gibbs farther south. The prominence of the peak indicates that the rock of the old roof pendant is less erodable than the younger light-gray granite of Kavanaugh Ridge extending down from the peak to the left. More metamorphics are visible on the ridge to the right and Camiaca Peak on the left. Between them, in an ice-hollowed basin, is Summit Lake.

MONO AND THE EASTERN SLOPE

Castles on the shore: Mono Lake's famed tufa towers were built when the lake level was higher and underwater springs deposited calcium carbonate and silica on the lake's floor.

(Opposite) Just as Yosemite Valley cannot be understood in isolation from what John Muir called the "glacial fountains" along the spine of the range, so the spine itself cannot be fully understood without reference to the precipitous east side of the range and the valleys beyond, even though these areas are outside the park boundary, which runs along the crest. As the Sierra rose in eons past, the valleys to the east were lowered, forming down-dropped blocks of the earth's crust and the precipitous fault scarp along the east side of the range. In the block directly east of Yosemite is Mono Lake, which is fed naturally by several east-side streams, including Lee Vining Creek at the left (coming down from Tioga Pass), and Dechambeau and Lundy Creeks at the right. The sphinx-like ridge of Mount Conness, on the park boundary, can be discerned at the upper left. Highway 395 skirts the base of the Sierra.

Mono Lake has risen and fallen many times during the geologic past, and ancient shorelines are clearly revealed on the snow-covered flats along the north shore. Pole Line Road, intersecting Highway 395 at the foot of the range, crosses these old shorelines.

(Opposite) Looking down Lundy Canyon to the east. Most of the Sierra streams that originally flowed into Mono Lake have been diverted into the Los Angeles aqueduct, causing the lake's level to drop some 40 feet in recent years. One result was that Negit Island, the smaller of the lake's two islands, was connected to the mainland at times of low water – a disaster for the great flocks of migratory birds that nested on the island in the spring. Coyotes and other predators were able to attack the nests. If the draining of the lake continues, it will diminish to about one-third of its present size, and a major Save-Mono-Lake campaign has been launched by environmentalists.

Tufa towers along Mono's south shore.

(Opposite) Since Negit Island has been joined to the mainland during the season of low water, the birds have abandoned it and have begun nesting on portions of the bottom exposed now as small islands. However, these too will become part of the mainland as the surface is lowered further.

Several old shorelines of Mono Lake are visible as concentric arcs along the beaches to the right. The flattened contours of Black Point indicate that it was a volcanic cinder cone that erupted underwater when the lake surface was much higher.

A sail on the lake develops a group of pictures of rare beauty and grandeur. Long ranks of snowy swans on the dark water, clouds of ducks enveloped in silvery spangles. The mighty barren Sierra rising abruptly from the waters to a height of 7000 feet, and stretching north and south for 20 miles with rows of snowy peaks…Snowfields and ice in the higher hollows, white torrents dashing down shadowy groves, and smooth moraine slopes drawn out upon the gray sage plains along the base of the range, with silvery streams descending in bright cheery song to vanish in the dry desert.

The larger island in the lake is about 2½ miles long, and is composed of hard lava and loose ashes. The smaller, half a mile long with a cone 240 feet high, is of hard black lava, quite recent. Boiling springs and hot jets of gas boil up from the lake-bottom near its shore…

The terraces visible as horizontal lines along the bottom of the Sierra fault scarp were cut by waves during the Ice Age when the surface was 800 feet higher than at present. On the left horizon are Mount Gibbs and Mount Dana, which on the far side overlook Tuolumne Meadows. The highest peak to the right is Mount Warren.

Volcano country south of Mono Lake, including some of the Mono Craters to the right and Wilson Butte, one of the Inyo Craters, in the foreground. All of the volcanoes in these deserts east of Yosemite have erupted in geologically recent times – some just a few hundred years ago – and are evidence of the continuing activity of forces deep in the earth, processes allied to those that elevated the Sierra and continue to do so.

(Opposite) Mammoth Mountain, accessible all winter from the south via Highway 395 through the desert east of the Sierra, is a mecca for Southern California skiers. Probably few are aware that they are sliding down a volcano that might erupt again some day. Recent earthquakes and hot-springs activity in the Mammoth area indicate potential eruptions somewhere in this region. However, the skiers are probably in less danger from an eruption than from breaking a leg; any volcanic action would give plenty of warning.

The June Mountain ski area, looking south in the distance down the east side of the Sierra across the Long Valley Caldera, site of a colossal eruption 700,000 years ago. Lake Crowley, a reservoir in the Los Angeles water system, is at the upper left.

(Opposite) Looking northwest over Mammoth Mountain, down into the canyon of the Middle Fork of the San Joaquin River and up to the dark metamorphic wall of the Minarets, Mount Ritter and Banner Peak. Most of this area was originally part of Yosemite National Park but was excluded when mineral deposits were discovered. However, it is now protected as the Minarets Wilderness, part of Inyo and Sierra national forests. The dark peak at the north end of the ridge is Mount Lyell, which is within the park, as is the snowy Clark Range at the upper left.

A closer view of the Minarets, culminating in the great massif of Ritter and Banner –all composed of dark metamorphic rock. Mount Lyell is at the far right. Buried in snow at the foot of the range are the fabulous lakes–Thousand Island and Garnet and Ediza.

(Opposite) Ritter, Banner, and part of the Minarets from the south.

YOSEMITE CURIOSITIES

Making your way through the mazes of the Coast Range to the summit of any of the inner peaks or passes opposite San Francisco, in the clear spring time, the grandest and most telling of all California landscapes is outspread before you. At your feet lies the great Central Valley, glowing golden in the sunshine… Along its eastern margin rises the mighty Sierra, miles in height, reposing like a smooth cumulus cloud in the sunny sky…

This view of the Sierra was taken from a Coast Range peak, Mount Copernicus, near Lick Observatory on Mount Hamilton, southeast of San Francisco. In the center of the picture is Half Dome, 120 miles away.

(Opposite) In the decades around the turn of the century a common way to prove your courage was to have your picture taken on Glacier Point's famed Overhanging Rock, 3000 feet above the valley floor. Some photographers, including Julius Boysen and George Fiske, made virtually a full-time job of setting up cameras on a ledge below and slightly west of the rock to photograph foolhardy visitors.

John Muir and friend on Overhanging Rock. The rough-riding outdoorsman on the left was an admirer of Muir's writings, and when he came West from the White House in 1903 one of his ambitions was to go camping with the mountaineer in Yosemite. Muir was reluctant to call off a trip of his own he had scheduled, so the President wrote him a plea: "I do not want anyone with me but you, and I want to drop politics absolutely for four days and just be out in the open with you."

Muir relented. The two set out by horseback from Wawona and camped near Glacier Point, where they woke up under three inches of snow. The President burst out of his blankets, snow flying, shouting "Bully!" Official photographers were waiting on Glacier Point and the two obligingly stood on Overhanging Rock. Later the President shouted to friends "This has been the bulliest day of my life!"

(Opposite) The dancing girl nearest the ledge of Overhanging Rock is Kitty Tatsch, an irrepressible practical jokester. On one occasion she upstaged the valley's annual Fourth-of-July parade by sitting on a haystack in a wheelbarrow which the valley blacksmith obligingly pushed along ahead of the formal procession. Unfortunately, in this picture taken on Overhanging Rock in 1900, the name of Kitty's brave dancing companion was not recorded for posterity.

The daredevil doing a handstand on the brink is reputed to be Douglas Fairbanks and the year was 1906, long before he became famous as Hollywood's greatest swashbuckler and acrobat in *Robin Hood* and *The Three Musketeers.* Doug appears twice because this is a stereopticon picture, made with a double lens. Peering through a stereopticon viewer at such pictures, a popular pastime around the turn of the century, you could see them in three dimensions. If you can focus your eyes in a special way, you can see this picture in 3D without the viewer. But don't try the handstand.

The National Park Service, fearing, with good reason, that ordinary mortals attempting to emulate Tatsch or Fairbanks would come to no good end, have barred access to the rock. Safety rails, warning signs, and stern rangers now keep visitors at a reasonable distance. Besides, the rock is getting older and could shear off at any time.

123

Sierra snow, for all its beauty, can be treacherous, as four Stanford students found out when they were caught on a ledge high on Mount Lyell at the end of March in 1958 and had to be rescued by an Army helicopter. The student farthest from the helicopter has evidently fallen in exhaustion, but all were safely flown to a hospital.

(Opposite) Mount Ritter and the Minarets, with Mono Lake visible through the notch.

These paintings, showing various stages in the evolution of Yosemite Valley, were made in the 1930s by Herbert A. Collins, Sr., and Herbert A. Collins, Jr. under the supervision of geologist Francois Matthes, who made the classic study of Yosemite for the United States Geological Survey. Although some details have been modified by later geological studies, in its main outlines the picture is accurate.

1. Some 15 million years ago Yosemite was a broad valley less than 1000 feet deep in a rising range of rolling hills. In a mild, rainy climate, the forests were mostly broad-leaf trees.

2. Continued uplift of this ancestral Sierra had speeded up the Merced River, and the valley was cut deeper into the growing range. The climate was cooler and drier, and the forests were mostly conifers, including sequoias.

3. At this stage the Sierra had been raised nearer its present height, and the Merced River was a torrent, eroding the canyon to a depth of 3000 feet.

4. By about one million years ago, the Yosemite glaciation had reached a climax, and the glacier reached far below the present valley to El Portal. This is known as the El Portal glaciation. Only the ridge of Clouds Rest, Half Dome, and a few other portions of the valley rim remained above the ice.

5. In the latest (Wisconsin) glaciation, the ice ended just below Bridalveil, where it left a pile of rock debris – a moraine – that later acted as a dam.

6. After the glaciers melted, perhaps as late as 10,000 years ago, the moraine impounded Lake Yosemite. Over the following millennia, the Merced River and its tributaries deposited deep beds of sediment in the lake and eventually filled it to the level of the present valley floor.

Yosemite became known to the world not only through the writings of John Muir and others but through the pictures of pioneer photographers such as Carlton E. Watkins and the work of landscape painters including Thomas Hill, Albert Bierstadt and William Keith. Hill, whose "Yosemite, 1889" appears here, was the most prolific of Yosemite's painters. He first visited the valley in 1862 (six years before Muir arrived) and made sketches that he later developed into giant oil landscapes. He had a studio in Yosemite Valley and later one in Wawona, where he presented Theodore Roosevelt with a Yosemite painting the President admired on his trip to visit Muir in 1903.

It was a moment of revelation on that bright spring day in 1868 when John Muir first stood on a summit of the Coast Range at Pacheco Pass and looked eastward in wonder across the San Joaquin Valley to the Sierra Nevada, "so gloriously colored and so luminous, it seemed not clothed with light but wholly composed of it, like the wall of some celestial city." He felt then that it should be called "not the Nevada or Snowy Range, but the Range of Light." A decade later he wrote:

After ten years of wandering and wondering in the heart of it, rejoicing in its glorious floods of light, the white beams of the morning streaming through the passes, the noonday radiance on the crystal rocks, the flush of the alpenglow, and the irised spray of countless waterfalls, it still seems above all others the Range of Light.

But those ten years also brought some disappointments and shocks as he watched the increasing human impact on the range and on Yosemite in particular. Four years before Muir arrived, President Lincoln had signed a bill granting Yosemite Valley to the state of California as a park, but few people in those days had any clear notion of what a mountain park should be. During Muir's early years in Yosemite the meadows of the valley had become barnyards, fenced and grazed, filled with cattle and horses and pigs, or plowed and planted to crops. In the high country the forests, including giant sequoias, were being devastated by loggers. In the summer great herds of sheep flocked into the mountain meadows and grazed them down to the roots.

One of Muir's favorite haunts was Shadow Lake (now known as Merced Lake), on the Merced River above Little Yosemite, where he discovered flowered meadows and groves of aspen that turned gold in the fall. He wrote:

I had told the beauty of Shadow Lake only to a few friends, fearing it might come to be trampled and "improved" like Yosemite. On my last visit, as I was sauntering along the shore on the strip of sand between the water and sod, reading the tracks of the wild animals that live there, I was startled by a human track, which I at once saw belonged to some shepherd…I began to fear that he might be seeking pasturage… Returning from the glaciers shortly afterward, my worst fears were realized. A trail had been made down the mountain-side from the north, and all the gardens and meadows were destroyed by a horde of hoofed locusts, as if swept by a fire. The money changers were in the temple.

It may have been at just such a moment that Muir consciously or unconsciously decided to abandon his life of free roaming in the mountains and take action to drive the money changers from the temple. He wrote:

The grass is eaten close and trodden until it resembles a corral…Nine-tenths of the whole surface of the Sierra has been swept by the scourge. It demands legislative interference.

To Muir's surprise and delight, publishers in New York and Boston were eager to print not only his stories of adventure in the mountains but his pleas for action to save the wilderness from devastation. By temperament he was a shy loner who shunned cities and crowds, but with increasing frequency he came down out of the mountains to do battle for the wilderness with writings and lectures. As a result several forest-preserve bills were introduced in Congress in the 1880s, and by 1890 bills were passed for the creation of Yosemite and Sequoia national parks.

Men and women inspired by the example of the crusading mountaineer gathered around him as a symbol, and in San Francisco in 1892 they organized the Sierra Club, with Muir as president. On that occasion a friend wrote:

I had never seen Mr. Muir so animated and happy before. Up to that time, Muir had been waging a continuous war against selfish commercial interests which would exploit and destroy the forests and beautiful regions of our state and nation, fighting in his early years in the state almost alone, with his back to the wall. Is it any wonder, then, that Muir saw in the Sierra Club the crystallization of the dreams and labor of a lifetime, an organization which would carry on the good work for generations to come?

The charter members of the club included a very large share of the leading citizens of California, including Adolph Sutro, Comstock tycoon and mayor of San Francisco; Charles F. Crocker, builder of the Southern Pacific Railroad; and President David Starr Jordan of Stanford. The club's first big battle was against the lumbermen and the cattle and sheep interests who sponsored a bill in Congress to cut the park's size by half. The bill passed the House but Muir and company persuaded the Senate to reject it. The park remained intact.

Next came the fight to plug a gigantic loophole in the bill creating Yosemite National Park. The park included some 700,000 acres of the high country around the valley, including Tuolumne Meadows and the Mariposa Big Trees, but the valley itself was left in the hands of the state of California, which had abused it from the beginning. For ten years Muir and the Sierra Club campaigned for "recession" of the valley to the federal government. The turning point came when Muir gained the ear of Theodore Roosevelt during their outing to Glacier Point in 1903. The President agreed, but the California Legislature still had to be persuaded. In a letter to a friend in 1905, Muir told of his adventures in politics:

I am now an experienced lobbyist; my political education is complete. Have attended Legislature, made speeches, explained, exhorted, persuaded every mother's son of the legislators, newspaper reporters, and everybody else who would listen to me.

The fight was won, both in Sacramento and later in Washington, where Muir had the help of Roosevelt and railroad magnate E. H. Harriman. The valley became part of the national park.

An even bigger battle loomed over the park's Hetch Hetchy Valley, which Muir called "the Tuolumne Yosemite" (see pages 84–87), coveted by San Francisco as a reservoir site. Muir's eloquent pen, which had reached lyrical heights in describing the wilderness, was capable of the wrath of a biblical prophet:

These temple destroyers, devotees of ravaging commercialism, seem to have a perfect contempt for Nature, and, instead of lifting their eyes to the God of the Mountains lift them to the Almighty dollar. Dam Hetch Hetchy! As well dam for watertanks the people's cathedrals and churches, for no holier temple has ever been consecrated by the heart of man.

This time Muir and the Sierra Club lost. A bill authorizing the damming of Hetch Hetchy was passed in 1913. Muir was crushed. A year later he died at 76.

But Muir's Sierra Club continued his battles, and over the years it played a leading role in the creation of other national parks, including Grand Canyon, Glacier, Kings Canyon, North Cascades, and Redwood, as well as a score of national seashores and national recreation areas.

Having seen Yosemite from above, we might find it enlightening to imagine how this region might have looked if Muir and his colleagues had failed, if there had been no national park. We would probably see the meadows of the valley and those of the Tuolumne fenced, grazed and planted. We might even see the valley obliterated under the waters of a reservoir like Hetch Hetchy. We would see the forests cut for timber and networks of logging roads over the high country, as well as mines and mining roads. Doubtless parts of the region would be as urbanized as the south shore of Lake Tahoe, with its high-rise hotels and casinos, its condominium subdivisions and traffic jams.

From this nightmare we have been spared by Muir and his followers. Our enjoyment of Yosemite, as it is now, might well be accompanied by a silent sense of inexpressible gratitude to the people, both famous and anonymous, who carried on the long battles to create and protect this park and who continue the struggle to preserve all the scenic splendors of the American continent.

The final section of this book is a pictorial reprise and summation of various themes that have been sounded here earlier. We invite you to enjoy each view creatively, without captions or commentary, experiencing only your own deepest responses. We extend the invitation in the spirit of John Muir's advice:

Climb the mountains and get their good tidings. Nature's peace will flow into you as sunshine flows into trees. The winds will blow their own freshness into you and the storms their energy, while cares will drop off like autumn leaves.

AHWAHNEE–The name of a large and important Indian village located near the mouth of Indian Canyon. The village gave its name, "Ahwahne" or "A-wa-ni," to the entire valley and the Indians of the valley became known as "Ahwahneechees."

BANNER PEAK–Willard D. Johnson, topographer for the U.S. Geological Survey, named the peak in 1883 for the cloud-banners streaming from the summit.

BIG OAK FLAT ROAD–The road takes its name from the village of Big Oak Flat, called after a famous oak (quercus lobata) whose trunk measured eleven feet in diameter. Starting at Knight's Ferry, the road reached Big Oak Flat in 1869 and was extended to the valley floor in 1874.

BRIDALVEIL FALL–Romantically named by Warren Baer, editor of the *Mariposa Democrat*, in 1856.

BRODERICK, MOUNT–David Broderick served as U.S. Senator from California and in 1859 was killed in San Francisco in a duel with Southern-sympathizer David S. Terry over issues leading to the Civil War.

BUNNELL POINT–Lafayette Bunnell was one of the first white men to enter the valley in 1851 as a member of the Mariposa Battalion pursuing Indians.

CAMP CURRY–Camp Curry (Curry Village) was started on June 1, 1899, by Mr. and Mrs. David Curry, who had been inspired to live an outdoor life while students under David Starr Jordan at the University of Indiana.

CATHEDRAL PEAK–Named by the Whitney geological survey in 1865.

CLARK, MOUNT–Named for Galen Clark, first guardian of Yosemite State Park, and the only man who could ever out-hike John Muir–as Muir himself said.

CLOUDS REST–The name recalls the timely retreat of Lafayette Bunnell and his party from the "Little Yosemite" when they saw clouds around the mountain peak indicating a coming snowstorm. Named in 1851.

CONNESS, MOUNT–As a state legislator, John Conness sponsored the bill creating the Geological Survey of California. Accordingly, a grateful Whitney geological survey named the mountain for him in 1864. As a U.S. senator, Conness sponsored in 1864 the bill by which Yosemite Valley and the Mariposa Grove were granted to California. "Conness" is accented on the second syllable.

DANA, MOUNT–James Dwight Dana, a professor of geology at Yale, was one of the founders of the modern science of geology in America. Named by the Whitney geological survey.

DUNDERBERG PEAK–Named by a member of the Army Corps of Engineers in 1878 for the mines of the same name on the north slope of the peak.

EL CAPITAN–Lafayette Bunnell says that he and his party named the great rock "El Capitan" as a Spanish translation of the Indian name "Tote-ack-ah-noola" derived from "ack," a rock, and "to-whon-e-o" meaning "chief."

ELLERY LAKE–Named for Nathaniel Ellery of Eureka, state engineer in charge of the extension of the Tioga Road from Tioga Pass to Mono Lake in 1909.

EL PORTAL–Spanish for "gateway" or "entrance" and applied by officers of Yosemite Valley Railroad Company around 1907.

FLORENCE, MOUNT–Named in 1886 for Florence Hutchings, the first white child born in Yosemite.

HALF DOME–Appropriately named by the Mariposa Battalion in 1851. The Indian name, "Tis-sa-ack," is said to have meant "cleft rock."

HETCH HETCHY–The name comes from a Miwok word for a grass with edible seeds once found abundantly in the now-flooded valley.

HOFFMANN, MOUNT–Named in 1863 by the Whitney geological survey for Charles F. Hoffmann, the survey's principal topographer.

ILLILOUETTE CANYON, CREEK, FALL–The name comes from the Indian name for the canyon, "Too-lool-a-we-ack," and is an example of how hard it was for white ears to catch the sounds of the Indian language.

JACK MAIN CANYON–Named for an old sheep-herder who ran sheep in the canyon for many years starting in the 1870s.

LEE VINING CREEK, PEAK, SETTLEMENT–Lee (Leroy) Vining came to California in 1852 and operated a sawmill on the creek named for him. Maps used a contracted form of the name, "Leevining," until 1957 when the Geographic Board decided that it should be two words.

LEMBERT DOME–Named in the 1890s for John Baptist Lembert, who homesteaded a quarter section of land near the dome in Tuolumne Meadows. Lembert raised Angora goats and collected botanical specimens which he sold to museums.

LIBERTY CAP–Named by Governor Leland Stanford in 1865 for its resemblance to the cap of Liberty on the half-dollar of the early 19th century.

LYELL, MOUNT–Brewer and Hoffmann of the Whitney survey named the peak in 1863 for the English geologist, Sir Charles Lyell, whose theories form the basis for modern geology. Lyell was Darwin's mentor. The name is accented on the first syllable.

MACLURE, MOUNT, FORK, CREEK, GLACIER, LAKE–The mountain was named by the Whitney geological survey in 1868 in honor of William Maclure, 1763-1840, a pioneer of American geology. In 1932 the Geographic Board applied the name to the other features. The name is sometimes incorrectly spelled "McClure."

MERCED RIVER, GROVE, PEAK, PASS, LAKE–A Spanish party exploring the San Joaquin Valley in 1806 expressed gratitude for finding the river after a long dry hike by naming it "El Rio de Nuestra Senora de la Merced,"–"The River of Our Lady of Mercy." John Muir called Merced Lake "Shadow Lake."

MIRROR LAKE–Fittingly named by C.H. Spencer of the Mariposa Battalion in 1851.

MONO LAKE–The name derives from a tribe of Shoshonean Indians who lived on both sides of the Sierra Nevada and were called "Monachi" by the neighboring Yokuts. The meaning of the word has been lost.

NEVADA FALL–"Nevada" means "snowy" in Spanish. Named in 1851 by Lafayette Bunnell who commented years later: "The white foaming water, as it dashed down Yo-wy-we (the Indian name of the fall) from snowy mountains, represented to my mind a vast avalanche of snow." (Bunnell: *The Discovery of the Yosemite*, 1880.)

NORTH DOME–The Mariposa Battalion applied the name in 1851. According to Lafayette Bunnell, the Indians called it "To-ko-ya," "The Basket."

RITTER, MOUNT–State geologist Josiah Whitney studied at the University of Berlin in the 1840s under Karl Ritter, one of the founders of scientific geography. In 1864 Whitney named the mountain in honor of his old professor.

SENTINEL ROCK–So named from its imagined resemblance to a gigantic watchtower.

SIERRA NEVADA–The name was applied to the range on April 3, 1776, by Father Pedro Font, who sighted the snowy peaks from a hill near the meeting of the Sacramento and San Joaquin rivers. The name is singular and the commonly heard versions, "Sierras" and "Sierra Nevadas," are technically incorrect. In Spanish "Sierra Nevada" denotes a range of mountains covered with snow.

STARR KING–Named during the Civil War for the Unitarian minister Thomas Starr King, who played an important part in keeping California in the Union. King visited Yosemite in 1860 and wrote a widely read series of articles on the valley.

TENAYA LAKE, CREEK, CANYON, PEAK–Lafayette Bunnell of the Mariposa Expedition named the lake for Chief Tenaya of the Ahwahneechee (Yosemite Valley) Indians in 1851. Chief Tenaya commented: "It already has a name. We call it 'Py-we-ack.'"

THREE BROTHERS–Three rocky peaks along the north wall of Yosemite Valley so named because the three sons of Chief Tenaya were captured near their base by the Mariposa Battalion.

TIOGA PASS, ROAD, PEAK, LAKE–Named after several mines bearing the name, "Tioga." The name comes from an Iroquois word meaning "where it forks," used as a place name in Pennsylvania and New York. Built by a mining company in 1882-3, the Tioga Road was bought by public subscription in 1915 and given to the government.

TUOLUMNE RIVER, CANYON, MEADOWS, FALLS, PEAK–The name derives from a tribe of Miwoks who lived along the lower Tuolumne and Stanislaus rivers in the San Joaquin Valley.

VERNAL FALL–The name comes from the Latin word for "spring" and was applied by Lafayette Bunnell of the Mariposa Battalion who first saw the fall on a spring day in 1851.

WATKINS, MOUNT–Carlton E. Watkins was an early photographer of Yosemite whose picture of Mirror Lake reflecting what is now Mount Watkins was extremely popular in the 1860s and led to the naming of the mountain for him.

WAWONA–Apparently derived from the local Indian word for "big tree," "woh-woh-nau," which itself was the imitation of the hoot of an owl, considered by the Indians as the guardian spirit of the big trees.

YOSEMITE–The name comes from a Miwok word meaning "grizzly bear." But whether the name was applied to the valley by outside tribes or whether it simply designated one village in the valley famous for its grizzly bear hunters is a matter of conjecture. Lafayette Bunnell of the Mariposa Battalion named the valley in 1851.

Ann Gilliam

Sources: *Place Names of the High Sierra* by Francis P. Farquhar and *California Place Names* by Erwin G. Gudde.

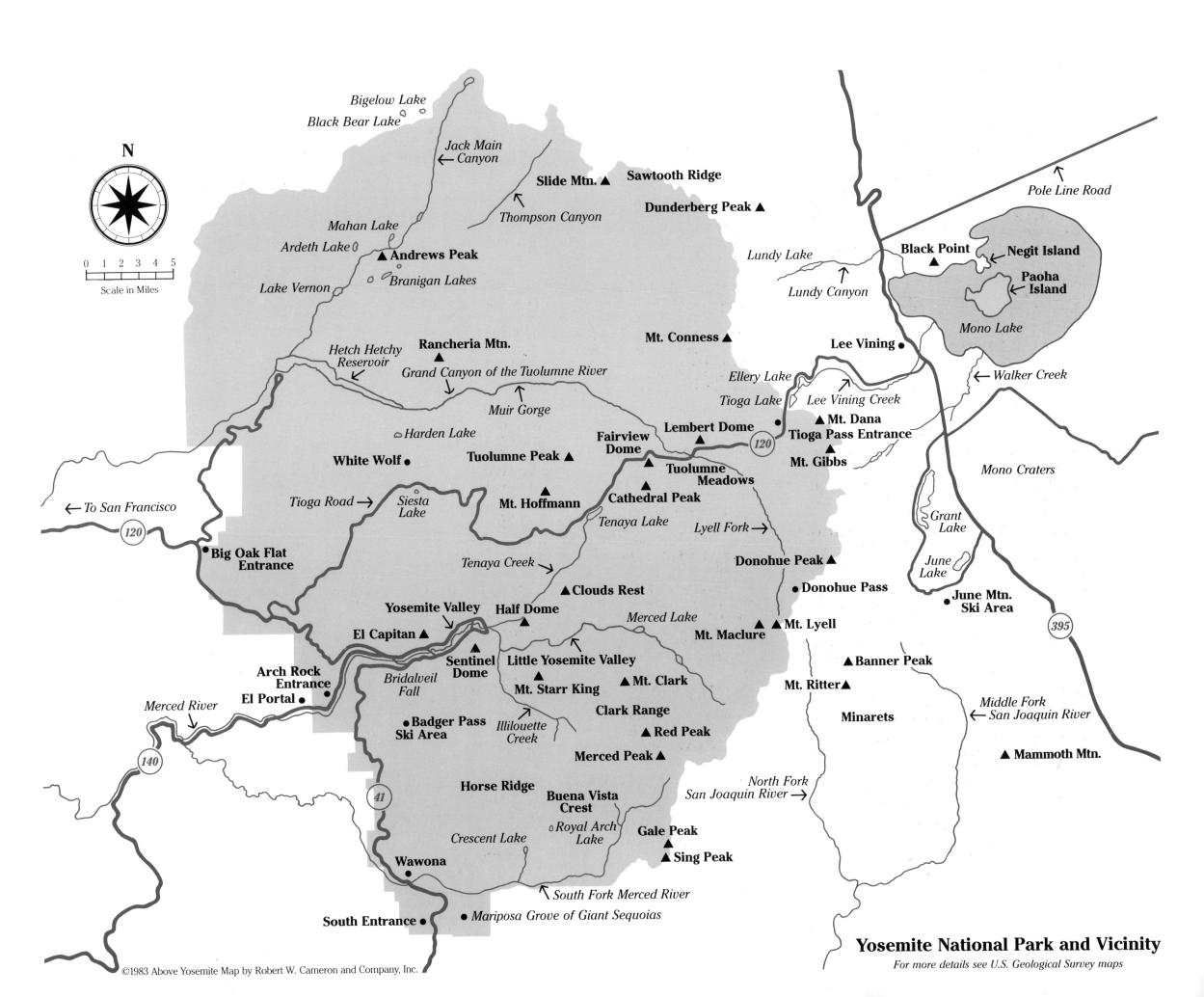

N

0 1 2 3 4 5
Scale in Miles

Bigelow Lake
Black Bear Lake
Jack Main
← Canyon
Slide Mtn. ▲   **Sawtooth Ridge**
Thompson Canyon   **Dunderberg Peak** ▲
Mahan Lake
Ardeth Lake   ▲ **Andrews Peak**
Lundy Lake   **Black Point**   **Negit Island**
▲
Lake Vernon   *Branigan Lakes*
Lundy Canyon   **Paoha Island**
Mono Lake
Hetch Hetchy   **Rancheria Mtn.**   **Mt. Conness** ▲   **Lee Vining** •
Reservoir   ▲
← Grand Canyon of the Tuolumne River
Ellery Lake   *← Walker Creek*
Muir Gorge   *Tioga Lake*   *Lee Vining Creek*
Harden Lake   **Lembert Dome**   ▲ **Mt. Dana**
Fairview   **Tioga Pass Entrance**
Dome   120
White Wolf •   **Tuolumne Peak** ▲   ▲   **Mt. Gibbs**
Tuolumne   *Mono Craters*
Meadows
Tioga Road →   *Siesta*   ▲ **Mt. Hoffmann**   **Cathedral Peak** ▲   *Grant*
← To San Francisco   *Lake*   *Lake*
120   *Tenaya Lake*   *Lyell Fork →*   *June*
Lake
Tenaya Creek →   **Donohue Peak** ▲
Big Oak Flat
Entrance •   **Clouds Rest** ▲   • **Donohue Pass**   • **June Mtn.**
Ski Area
Yosemite Valley   **Half Dome**   *Merced Lake*
El Capitan ▲   ▲   ▲ **Mt. Lyell**   395
Mt. Maclure
Sentinel   **Little Yosemite Valley**
Arch Rock   **Dome**   ▲ **Banner Peak**
Entrance   *Bridalveil*   **Mt. Starr King** ▲   **Mt. Clark** ▲
El Portal •   *Fall*   **Clark Range**   **Mt. Ritter** ▲
Merced River   **Badger Pass**   *Illilouette*   **Minarets**
• **Ski Area**   *Creek*   ▲ **Red Peak**   *Middle Fork*
← San Joaquin River
Merced Peak ▲
140   **Horse Ridge**   *North Fork*   ▲ **Mammoth Mtn.**
41   **Buena Vista**   *San Joaquin River →*
Crest
Crescent Lake   *Royal Arch*
Lake   **Gale Peak**
▲
Wawona •   ▲ **Sing Peak**
South Fork Merced River
South Entrance •   • *Mariposa Grove of Giant Sequoias*

©1983 Above Yosemite Map by Robert W. Cameron and Company, Inc.

Yosemite National Park and Vicinity
For more details see U.S. Geological Survey maps